Roman Mythology

A Guide to Roman History, Gods, and Goddesses

Jordan Parr

Table of Contents

Introduction 1

Chapter One: Pax Deorum 3

Chapter Two: Lightning Bolts and Sea Foam 7

Chapter Three: Kings, Wolves, and Destiny 21

Chapter Four: Hair Made of Snakes 31

Chapter Five: Impossible Tasks and Magnificent Champions 40

Final Words 51

Introduction

"Let others praise ancient times.
I am glad I was born in these."

- Ovid (43 BCE - 17 CE)

When famed Roman poet Ovid wrote these words over two millennia ago, he was voicing a preference for his own time (which, to him, was modern) while waving away any nostalgia for times long past. Reading his words now, of course, his time is as far removed from us as those "ancient times" were from him. It's a poignant reminder that our lives will eventually be history, too--and it also speaks to the ever-present human longing for an ancient, storied past. Perhaps Ovid would forgive our curiosity about ancient times if he knew that Rome's past is still everywhere in our present despite the thousands of years gone by. Rome continues to captivate our imaginations. Its gods, heroes, and monsters appear everywhere, from children's books to famous paintings to company logos. There are traces of its mythology in our language, in the way we mark the passing of time (for example, January, like its namesake the two-headed god Janus) and in the planets that move through our skies (where Jupiter, king of the gods, still looms large). Though the Roman Empire has been gone for centuries, its hold on Western culture never truly disappeared.

Roman mythology is closely linked in our minds to Greek mythology, and for a good reason. As Rome evolved into an empire, its people began to long for a mythical history to solidify Roman identity. Romans, however, were not particularly interested in the effort it would take to create these myths from scratch, so they borrowed them. Greece was not the only influence on Roman culture, but it was the most prominent one. The overlap between the two mythologies can lead people to group them together and assume their differences are insignificant. Still, when the Romans appropriated these tales, they made them their own, renaming the leading players and infusing the stories with a good dose of Roman ideology. Crucially, Roman religion and myth were meant to be practical. They discarded the Greeks' affinity for poetry and philosophy and instead focused on structure and ceremony--the gods' stories became Rome's stories, providing a divine pedigree for its conquerors and the proper rituals for continued prosperity. In Rome, the gods, like everything else, existed to benefit the empire.

This book will introduce you to those gods, to the heroes they helped (and hindered), to the monsters they created and killed, and to the world of ancient Rome where they were worshipped. The stories are not for the faint of heart. They are full of war and betrayal, of blood and sorrow, of long voyages and narrow escapes, and most of all, of the perilous thrill that awaits mortals that venture into the realm of the gods. As you read, take to heart the well-worn Latin proverb, *"audentes fortuna juvat,"* or, as we better know it, "fortune favors the brave."

Chapter One: Pax Deorum
How Romans Practiced Religion

In modern society, especially in Western civilization, since the spread of the Abrahamic religions (Christianity, Judaism, and Islam), we tend to associate religion and spirituality with morality. A primary function of a god, in our view, is to sit as a moral authority who will judge us for our wrongs and reward us for our virtues. This concept of divinity does not exist in Roman society. The gods of ancient Rome were rarely paragons of righteousness, instead often succumbing to pettiness or anger just as any human might. A Roman might consider a god above them, but the hierarchy was based on power, not purity. And therefore, the relationship between a Roman and the gods was transactional, in which prayers and sacrifices were made not in supplication but to gain a god's favor. The Roman religious ideal was the *pax deorum* (meaning divine peace or pact), in which a satisfied deity aided mortals in obtaining their desires.

How do you satisfy a god? If you're Roman, it's a simple trade. You request the god in question, promising them something for their troubles--perhaps food, wine, or a blood sacrifice. If the god held up their end of the deal, you held up yours. As time went on, the rules for these transactions became codified into a set of divine laws (the *jus divinum*). In addition to individual bargains struck with the gods, Roman society as a whole would seek divine benevolence. Gods were consulted before battle and celebrated during religious festivals. Praying to the gods on behalf of Rome was an official civic position. And unlike the formless or unknowable gods of some religions, Roman gods behaved remarkably like humans in their conflicts and appetites. They fell prey to love and anger, lust and jealousy, and even hunger--it was common to have a place at the table and a portion of food for a god during festival meals. The concept of gods who behaved like humans was strongly influenced by Greek myths, but the ritualistic and somewhat perfunctory way Romans structured their relationship with these gods was very Roman.

Reading the Entrails: The Structure of Roman Religion

To reiterate, Roman religion was not one of individual or even societal morality. There was no passion in the worship of the gods. In fact, religious passion was often seen as a threat in a world where a citizen's loyalty was expected to lie with the Roman state. Religion was not a place for emotions or opinions but rather a series of tasks to be carried out. The gods did not care if your heart was in the right place. They generally did not care about your heart at all. They only cared that you performed the rites and rituals correctly. For this, Rome developed the jus divinum to guide religious practice and public officiants responsible for performing rites on a national level. Two prominent types of officiants were the priest and the augur.

Most of us are familiar with the idea of priests as the leaders of religious movements or organizations, but this was not their function in ancient Roman life. Roman priests were educated in a special institution (the collegium pontificum) and employed by the state to perform sacrifices and other rituals. The highest of these offices was held by a married couple, the rex and regina sacrorum, who would serve the Roman state in this capacity from the time of their appointment until they died.

The Roman augur is akin to a diviner or soothsayer. Instead of giving the gods offerings, an augur's job was to determine their will. They worked to interpret the omens that were believed to be divine messages sent to mortals. When guidance was needed for specific situations, an augur could perform rituals for greater clarification, the most common of these being sacrificing an animal and then reading its entrails. This type of divination came to Rome from the Etruscans (a civilization in what is now northern Italy absorbed by the Roman Empire), who were perhaps second only to the Greeks in their influence of Roman religion.

The Roman Melting Pot

While it is easiest to pick out the strong influences of Greek and Etruscan cultures on Roman religion and mythology, it is important to note that Rome was influenced by nearly all the cultures it came into contact with--which, considering Rome was in the business of conquering as many places as it could, was a lot of cultures. The Roman way was not to convert conquered territories to any particular religion (remember, religion was not a matter of personal conviction to the Romans), but rather to absorb all things into itself, allowing conquered territories to continue with their own practices. Other nameable influences include mythology from Egypt and other Middle Eastern cultures, and then, of course, the eventual rise (after much persecution) of Christianity. Up until the emperors themselves became Christians and committed to spreading the good word, the Roman state was uninterested in evangelizing, instead opting for a laissez-faire approach that allowed for the practices of many cultures to mingle.

This kind of polytheistic religious free-for-all was part of Roman society from the beginning. Early Romans, living in a predominantly agricultural society, believed that all parts of the world had their own spirit (a practice called animism). This included natural elements like trees and bodies of water, as well as human-made places like buildings. This is, perhaps, the root of the transactional nature of Roman religion--make a spirit happy, and it will help you. You might get rain for your crops from the spirit in your land or protection for your family from the spirit in your house. Over time, cults would form around certain spirits, and this devotion would be transferred to the gods that would be adopted as Rome grew into an empire with a national narrative.

Even as Rome came to collectively worship gods such as Jupiter, Juno, and Minerva, individual families would continue to worship their own household gods. A type of spirit called a lar was believed to protect each household so long as the family remembered to keep it happy with rituals and offerings. One such offering was part of every meal, given to the household spirit by throwing it into the fire. Special rites might be performed to ask for aid or favor during significant life events. In addition to the leading household spirit, there might be other spirits assigned to very particular parts of the household (one of these are the penates, who were amusingly responsible for a household's pantry).

There were other divine beings in the Roman world, most of them living in the space between the private sphere of the household god and the empire-wide domain of the larger gods. It was common for a city to affiliate itself with a god, building temples and statues in honor of that god and making sacrifices to them. Figures like Bacchus, Cybele, and Isis (borrowed from Egyptian mythology) had their own cults dedicated to them. You could even find shrines built in places where roads crossed because it was believed that a crossroad was a common gathering spot for spirits. In this, you can see Roman pragmatism at work--after all, why lose a chance to gain favor with a god?

Chapter Two: Lightning Bolts and Sea Foam
Roman Gods and Goddesses

Nearly all the deities in Roman mythology take their backstories from their Greek counterparts. Still, it isn't entirely accurate to say that Romans only adopted the Greek gods and renamed them. Many of the gods that populated the pantheon of ancient Rome already existed, but they lacked compelling narratives. The Romans merged these gods with the stories from Greek myths, weaving their own religious history into this foreign scaffolding to create a new mythology for themselves.

Jupiter, King of the Gods

With his flashy lightning bolts and command of the skies, it is difficult to look at Jupiter and not see his Roman counterpart Zeus (he also shares quite a few similarities with the Norse god of thunder, Thor). But Jupiter began as a god of farmers, who only later became the legend who cast out his own father, Saturn (more on him later), to become the ruler of the gods and Rome's chief deity. Jupiter's transformation from an elemental god responsible for a bountiful harvest to a warrior god with an epic origin story mirrors Rome's path from an agricultural society to a famed and seemingly unstoppable empire.

Jupiter was one of a trio of gods with temples on Rome's Capitoline Hill; the other two temples changed hands, but Jupiter's was always his. Along with lightning bolts, Jupiter was associated with oak trees and eagles. Interpreting the actions of eagles was thought to be the best way to divine omens from Jupiter. Through the centuries, Jupiter has maintained his kingly presence in many ways, perhaps most famously in giving his name to the largest planet in our galaxy.

Juno, Goddess of the Moon

Juno was another of Saturn's children. When her brother, Jupiter, overthrew their father, she helped him. She then married him (the Roman gods were not squeamish about incest). Effectively the queen of the gods, she was the patron goddess of Rome. She was also the goddess of fertility, childbearing, and marriage--although her marriage to Jupiter was plagued with strife (one myth has Jupiter as the creator of fog, which he used as cover to hide his infidelity from Juno). Any aspect of life that Romans believed to be women's work or domain was watched over by Juno.

Juno wore a diadem befitting her position in the pantheon and was sometimes seen in a veil or a goatskin cloak. Occasionally, she was shown in armor or with weapons. Though Jupiter ruled the skies, the moon belonged to Juno. It was linked to her as it was linked to the cycles of nature, both of them representing the way life ebbs, flows, and repeats. Thus, she was seen as a goddess of change and transformation, fluidity, and light in the darkness.

Saturn, Architect of Earth's Golden Age

Saturn has perhaps the most turbulent path of the Roman gods. His story begins with a triumph, when he defeated his despotic father, Uranus, and took over the cosmos. However, the power soon went to Saturn's head, and he became quite the despot himself. To prevent a prophecy that one of his sons would overthrow him as he had overthrown his father, he decided to eat all of his children as soon as they were born (yes, really). Understandably fed up with this kind of behavior, his wife, Ops, hid their son Jupiter from Saturn, giving him a rock instead. Eating the rock made Saturn throw up all the children he had eaten, who then joined Jupiter to kick Saturn out of heaven.

Strangely, Saturn seemed to have learned his lesson because his expulsion from heaven landed him on earth, where he decided to teach humankind how to farm benevolently. His reign on earth is known as the "Golden Age," and supposedly, all people were treated as equals during that time. This part of Saturn's story is a Roman invention, not found in the story of Saturn's Greek counterpart Cronus. It was also the basis of the festival Saturnalia, a solstice celebration of gift-giving and merriment in which slaves were allowed to eat with their masters, and a commoner was crowned as king of the festival. (Saturnalia was one of many mid-winter festivals that would see some of its traditions incorporated into Christmas.)

Neptune, Sovereign of the Seas

Neptune was another son of Saturn, one of the children his father devoured and then regurgitated. After helping Jupiter dispose of his father, he became the god of the seas (as well as other moving bodies of water like springs and rivers). He was also the god of storms, earthquakes, and horses. He lived beneath the Mediterranean Sea in a golden palace with the sea goddess Salacia and their children, and as long as he stayed in the sea, his power was almost limitless. Anyone whose life or livelihood was related to the oceans was familiar with making offerings to Neptune for good fortune.

Neptune was commonly portrayed with a trident (a three-pronged spear used for both fishing and as a weapon), and he was often riding on a chariot pulled by dolphins, horses, or sea horses. If you provoked his displeasure or lost his good favor while sailing in his oceans, he might agitate the waters, sinking your ship and drowning you. However, the most legendary use of his power is in a story from Ovid, in which he gets too excited and creates a flood that covers the whole earth. The waters are finally called back to the sea by Neptune's son

Triton sounding his conch, leaving only two people alive to repopulate the earth.

Pluto, Ruler of the Underworld

Like his Roman parallel Hades, Pluto is most famous for his dominion over the world of the dead deep underground. Given his power over subterranean spaces, it is less well known that he was also the god of all things mined from those spaces, including precious metals and gemstones, and therefore often considered responsible for wealth and material good fortune. Unlike his brothers on their thrones or in their golden palaces, Pluto seemed happy to keep to his dark home under the earth with his three-headed dog, with one notable exception which turned out to affect the whole world.

Pluto, the unwitting recipient of an arrow from the god Cupid, fell in love with Proserpina, daughter of Jupiter and Ceres (and his niece). He kidnapped her and took her to the underworld to be his bride. Ceres, who was responsible for animal fertility and crops, became so distraught at her daughter's disappearance that she forgot to keep things growing. This eventually became catastrophic, of course, and finally, the other gods insisted that Pluto let Proserpina go. Pluto was able to insist that Proserpina was tied to the underworld on a technicality (she had eaten pomegranate seeds while there), and so, a compromise was reached that Proserpina would spend half her time with Pluto in the underworld and half her time on earth with her mother. In Roman mythology, Proserpina's absence from her mother is the reason plants die and animals hibernate in the autumn and winter.

Minerva, Mighty of Mind

Minerva is unique among the Roman gods for several reasons. While she eventually became associated with the Greek goddess of wisdom, Athena, she originally came to Roman mythology as the Etruscan goddess Menrva. As the goddess of wisdom, she was the most clever and calculating of all the gods, perhaps because she was born directly out of Jupiter's forehead. (In some versions of the story, this is because Jupiter impregnated her mother Metis and then feared his child would usurp him as he had Saturn. To prevent this, he swallowed Metis with Minerva in utero, but Minerva grew inside him.)

In addition to being the goddess of wisdom, Minerva was also the goddess of commerce, industry, education, crafts and artisans, doctors, musicians, and warfare. Her association with warfare grew with the empire, and in later centuries she was often depicted in armor and holding a spear. Unlike her brother Mars, also a god of war, invoking Minerva's aid on the battlefield was not about strength, but strategy. And perhaps unique among all the gods, Minerva was famously uninterested in romance or sex. She refused all offers of companionship in favor of her own brilliant company.

Mars, Bringer (and Ender) of War

Like his father, Jupiter, Mars started as a farming god. (This association remains in language, where he gave his name to March, the month that brings us spring.) However, he later and more famously became a god of war, perhaps *the* god of war, as his long-lasting association with the red planet that bears his name can attest. (In paintings, Mars usually has red skin.) Romans made offerings to Mars before they went into battle, sacrificing rams, bulls, pigs, and sometimes horses at his altar. However, Mars was not simply a force of strength or violence, as his guidance in war was believed to bring resolution to conflict, followed by lasting peace. For this reason, though he carried a spear, it was always adorned with the laurel of peace.

Mars was also considered a protector, not just of men in war but, perhaps due to his agricultural origins, of animals against injury or sickness. He was also the father of Romulus, the founder of Rome. This connection of Rome's beginning with Mars' lineage is one of the clearest examples of how Roman mythology offered not just a religious structure but also gave the Roman Empire a history that felt worthy of its continual conquests. Though often shown naked, he also at times wore military gear, including a breastplate with the severed head of a gorgon on it. The head of a defeated gorgon (a fearsome creature that could turn men to stone) was thought to protect its bearer.

Venus, Protectress of Love and Lovers

In tamer versions of the birth of Venus, she is the child of Jupiter and Dione, one of his many mistresses. However, a wilder and more brutal tale has often caught people's imaginations: when Saturn overthrew his father Uranus, he also castrated him, and blood from this wound fell into the sea, causing Venus to be born from the foam that formed. This story has inspired many works of art, among them Botticelli's very famous "The Birth of Venus," where Venus rises from the sea on an open clam. Another well-known story is that of Mars and Venus, who had a torrid, on-again, off-again love affair--complementary forces of love and war.

The goddess of love and desire, Venus, was almost always portrayed as a young woman, usually naked and often seen with roses, myrtle, and seashells. Mars was not her only lover--she had many of both genders, and her association with love and sex made her the patron of not only lovers but prostitutes. Just as Rome's founder Romulus was supposedly the son of Mars, many of Rome's noble families claimed Venus as an ancestor, showing, once again, how Roman mythology was seen as not just a belief system but had woven itself into Roman ideas and history.

Cupid, Archer of Fate

Another god of love and desire, Cupid, found his way into quite a few of his fellow gods' stories due to his defining power: a quiver of arrows that could cause their target to become either enamored or repulsed. As mentioned above, it was Cupid's arrow that caused Pluto to fall in love with Proserpina, setting off a chain of events that altered the seasons forever. Another often-told story was that of Apollo and Daphne: Cupid, annoyed with Apollo for teasing him about his archery skills (or, in some stories, the size of his arrows), shoots Apollo with one of his golden arrows so that Apollo would fall in love with the next being he saw. That being was Daphne, and Cupid promptly shot Daphne with a leaden arrow, making her, depending on who you ask, either impervious to love at all or repulsed by Apollo specifically.

Adding to Cupid's romantic credentials is his parentage. He was commonly believed to be the son of Venus, often through her torrid affair with Mars (though Mercury, Vulcan, and Jupiter were also candidates for Cupid's father). Even Cupid's name is about love and desire, being taken from the Latin words cupere, meaning "to desire," and cupido, meaning "lust." He was often portrayed with his bow and arrows, a young man or even a child, and sometimes with wings (because, of course, love is eternally youthful and flighty).

Vulcan, the Ugly God Who Made Beauty with Fire

Like Cupid, Vulcan's name also illustrates his primary qualities. His name comes from the Latin word vulcanus, which also gave us the term "volcano." *Vulcanus* means fire, and fire was Vulcan's purview, both in its ability to destroy and its power to create. This is why Vulcan is also the god of blacksmiths and craftsmen and is often depicted with a hammer or other metalwork tools or artisanry. He was also a brilliant god, though his wisdom wasn't always put to the noblest of uses, particularly when it came to his wife, Venus. Venus was forced into marriage with Vulcan by Jupiter, with some versions claiming that Jupiter acted because Vulcan had captured Juno and refused to release her unless Venus married him. Unable to make Venus love him, he became vindictive and created a strong but invisible net that he used to ensnare Venus and her lover Mars, catching them in their affair and then calling the other gods to laugh at their nakedness.

You could say Vulcan's cruelty was earned honestly, though, for as a child, he was cast out of Mt. Etna, the beautiful mountain where the gods dwelled. Vulcan himself was not beautiful. He was called the ugliest of the gods and often portrayed as lame. In some stories, these physical imperfections are the result of his fall from the mountain; in others, his father Jupiter or his mother Juno threw him off of Mt. Etna because his appearance repulsed them. Vulcan grew up alone, and when he found his way back to the mountain, it was not to an airy peak but deep underground. A cave led Vulcan to the fiery heart of Mt. Etna, which became the forge where he learned his craft and created such wonders as Mercury's helmet and Jupiter's lightning bolts.

Apollo, Shining Patron of Music and Medicine

Like the other gods in this chapter, much of Apollo's characteristics and story were adapted from the Greeks. However, unlike the other gods, Apollo was never renamed and went by the same name in Roman mythology as he does in Greek mythology. Apollo had many functions as a god--he was the god of the sun, light, and prophecy, of music, poetry, medicine, and science, and patron of doctors, law, justice, peace, and reason. As the god of medicine, Apollo was thought to bring healing, and by some accounts, was introduced to Rome so he could bring about an end to the city's plague. However, this also meant that if you fell out of favor with Apollo, he might curse you with disease.

Born to Jupiter and Latona (Leto in the Greek myths) and his twin sister, Diana, Apollo was usually portrayed with a lyre to symbolize his love of music or a bow and arrow, as he was also a great archer. He was also often shown in a halo of light, which symbolized not only his association with the sun but also the divine enlightenment he gifted to those in his favor. He was almost always shown as young and virile and was known to take lovers of both genders.

Diana, Huntress of the Forest

The Romans borrowed many elements of Diana from her Greek counterpart Artemis, but she may have started as an early Roman forest god. She was represented as a young woman with a bow flanked either by trusty hounds or by nimble deer. These two animals, the hound, and the deer reflected the duality contained within Diana. She was a goddess of domestic and wild animals, of not just the forest but also the hunt. The duality of her nature was extended in her association with both chastity and fertility. She was also known as a protector to women in childbirth, a link that may have come from the story that she assisted her mother Latona with the birth of her twin brother Apollo just days after being born herself.

Diana was also associated with the moon, particularly the harvest moon, and was known not only as forever young and pretty but an avowed virgin--any attempts at romancing her would often provoke her notable temper. A temple at Ephesus, in what is modern-day Turkey, was dedicated to Artemis/Diana and was once one of the seven wonders of the world. Her temple in Rome was a place of refuge for slaves, who could seek sanctuary there.

Bellona, Bloody Battle Goddess

Though she is also linked to the Greek Enyo, Bellona is another deity with early Roman roots. It is possible settlers from the ancient Sabine tribe brought Bellona to Rome. After a time, she became incorporated into the established Pantheon, sometimes said to be another child of Jupiter and Juno, and at times linked romantically with Mars. Her name comes from the Latin word for warfare, *bellum*, so as you might guess, she is a goddess of war. Unlike Minerva with her strategy or Mars, whose presence promised peace after war, Bellona was the patroness of the frenzied, violent parts of war. Her favor was elicited to bring Romans the kind of fervor and passion in battle that would terrify their enemies.

Her relationship with the more brutal side of war was reflected in depictions of her, where she wore armor and bore a spear and torch, or (according to Virgil) a kind of whip called a scourge, which was covered in blood. Perhaps most violent of all were the early practices of her priests, who mutilated their own bodies to offer her their blood, and possibly might have engaged in human sacrifice as well.

Vesta, the Sacred Flame

Vesta, another child that Saturn devoured and then threw up, is perhaps not as well-known as her siblings, but even today, many people are familiar with the name of her followers, the vestal virgins. Vesta was the goddess of domesticity and the hearth specifically, and her temple housed a divine flame that had to be kept burning at all times. The vestal virgins were responsible for this flame; a vestal virgin was chosen at age six and began serving in the temple when she turned ten. She was not allowed to marry or have sex throughout her 30 years of service, on the penalty of death.

Vesta was a fixture in Rome from its early days, as King Numa, the second ruler of Rome, founded a cult for her during his reign. Vesta shares much with the Greek goddess Hestia, but while Hestia was also associated with an undying fire, no separate class of citizens was dedicated to tending it. The most common portrayal of Vesta was not her person but her sacred flame. However, at times she was also depicted as a woman wearing drapes and a veil.

Ceres, Creator of Seasons

Ceres, goddess of fertility, agriculture, and the harvest, is most well-known for her part in the story of her daughter Proserpina's abduction by Pluto. Ceres's grief overwhelmed her, and she let nature begin to die, therefore establishing the seasons. However, Ceres was an extremely popular goddess in her own right and had her own annual festival. Ceres is the only one of the twelve main Roman gods connected to agriculture (while Jupiter and Mars both had begun as agricultural gods, they lost these aspects as they became more popular). She was also part of a trio with the wine gods, Liber and Libera, called the Aventine Triad.

There are several versions of the relationship between Ceres and humanity in mythology. In one, she is the god who taught humans how to grow and harvest grains; in another, humanity was dying of starvation, and she saved them with her harvest. This strong association with crops and the harvest led to her being portrayed carrying grain or wearing a crown made out of wheat. A daughter of Saturn, Ceres was the fifth of Jupiter's siblings who joined to overthrow their father.

Mercury, the Winged Messenger

Mercury, often said to be the son of Jupiter from his affair with the nymph Maia, was the god of travel, commerce, communication, and all kinds of movement. As messenger for the gods and guide to dead souls, he possessed unique freedom and mobility. His powers allowed him to journey even to the underworld, access that no other god besides Pluto shared. He also wore a magical helmet, made by Vulcan, which had wings and allowed him to fly. In early days he was the god of profits and trade, leading to his association with merchants, but he was also known as a trickster, which made him patron to thieves as well.

Because he could go anywhere and was privy to all the correspondence between gods, he was something of a gossip. He was often the one whispering secrets about one god in the ear of another. It was Mercury who discovered the affair between Venus and Mars, and it was also Mercury who finally found Proserpina hidden away in the underworld. Mercury was incorporated into broader Roman religious practices as the father of the lares (household deities). More recently, he has been invoked in pop culture through the DC character The Flash, who moves at incredible speeds and wears a headpiece with wings on it.

Janus, the God with Two Faces

Janus is one of the few Roman gods with no Greek equivalent. With two faces that looked in opposite directions, he was able to know both the past and the future (a power he shared with the Etruscan god Culsans). He was the god of transitions, of gates and doors and other openings where people passed from one space to the next. Because of this association with entrances and exits, he was also seen as the god of beginnings and endings. And as the god of beginnings, he was often the first god to be named in a Roman's prayer, even before Jupiter.

Because he saw into all of time, he was believed to be wise and able to bless his followers with wisdom. He was also called upon in times of change and sometimes known to be the one who caused those changes, which is perhaps why his festival was celebrated at the beginning of the calendar year (and why his name is found in that of the first month, January). Not to be left out of Rome's favorite pastime, he also had a part to play in war: a gate bearing his name stood at the entrance to the forum. While times were peaceful, the gate stayed closed, but when Rome declared war, they opened Janus's gate to send forth the power of Rome mystically.

Bacchus, the Divine Merrymaker

Bacchus and his Greek parallel Dionysus have remained fairly well entrenched in popular consciousness, perhaps due to continuously being referenced in art, poetry, music, and literature--and maybe a little bit because people love an excuse to have a good time. The god of wine, ecstasy, and ritual madness, he was also known to dabble in fertility (lust for life), agriculture (especially the growing of grapes for wine), and theatre (what's a good time without entertainment?). Portrayals of Bacchus varied. At times, he was a drunken man. At others, he was a youth clothed only in vines and grapes, and occasionally he was a child with curls and a glass of wine. His symbols were grapes, wine, and an exceptional staff called a thyrus, wrapped in leaves and topped with a pinecone.

Bacchus, party lover that he was, seldom went anywhere alone but was often accompanied by both human women and nymphs, as well as half-human, half-goat satyrs. A popular god, his popularity was eventually considered by the Roman Senate to threaten the state. Senators were also suspicious of the rites of Bacchanalia, as they were performed in secret and could therefore be a cover for political scheming. For this reason, Bacchanalia was eventually banned in Rome, and the cult of Bacchus suppressed.

Faunus, Horned God of Nature

Most of the Roman gods were portrayed with human bodies, but Faunus was almost always shown as half-human (the top half) and half goat (the bottom half) and having horns on his head. He was the god of nature, including woods, fields, and wilderness. He was also the patron god of shepherds, believed not only to protect flocks but to control their fertility. If flocks were not fertile enough, the Romans thought Faunus was shirking his responsibilities and would beat his statue to get his attention. Faunus was not as entangled with Jupiter's family tree as many gods, but he was occasionally said to be the son of Saturn or of Mercury.

Faunus was also associated with a good harvest, and his festival was celebrated in December. There are not many stories involving Faunus, but one of the more famous is his pursuit of the nymph Syrinx, who begged the river god to be turned into reeds so she could avoid him. This did not deter Faunus, who cut down the reeds and made them into an instrument, called either the Syrinx or the pan pipes (after Faunus' Greek equivalent Pan).

Chapter Three: Kings, Wolves, and Destiny
Roman Heroes and Demigods

The gods and goddesses of Rome were powerful and intriguing, but they were not the only figures in Roman religion and mythology. Along with the less powerful types of supernatural creatures like the satyrs, nymphs, and household spirits, there were also the humans that became entangled with the affairs of the gods. At times, the relationship between humans and gods was benevolent, as when the gods gave humanity knowledge or gifts. At other times, things were more complicated, such as when gods fell in love with mortals and had children with them.

These children were demigods, half-human and half-divine, and often the stars of some of the most famous Roman myths. Most Roman heroes could be traced back to a divine lineage. The line between myth and history is complicated even for modern scholars due to the destruction of Rome's historical records by the Gauls in the fourth century. Beyond historical accuracy, however, this blurring of legend and history is yet another illustration of how Roman religion worked to legitimize--in Roman eyes, at least--their right to go forth and conquer the world.

Aeneas, the Trojan Warrior

The story of Troy is well-known, not only through numerous retellings in books and films but as the ultimate cautionary tale about being tricked by duplicitous enemies. After the Greeks invaded Troy with their wooden horse, the city fell. However, Aeneas and his men escaped because he was no ordinary soldier, but the son of the goddess Venus. It was Venus's warning and help that allowed him to escape.

Aeneas is one of the most famous demigods in Roman mythology, as his identity was tied not only to Venus but to the founding of Rome.

His father, Anchises, was a Trojan royal who was seduced by Venus while wandering near Mt. Ida, and Aeneas was actually left in the care of the nymphs who lived in the mountains there as a child. Eventually, Aeneas was taken by his father to live in Troy, until the Greeks attacked and Aeneas began a fabled journey that would later be woven into the history of Rome itself. The most prominent chronicler of Aeneas's story was the poet Virgil, who made it the subject of his poem *The Aeneid*. Establishing the story of Aeneas and linking it to Rome was a crucial part of establishing Rome's history and culture separate from the Greeks, as Aeneas was a celebrated enemy of the Greeks who still had ties to the gods. Because of this, Aeneas was not only invoked as a father of Rome the city but was also claimed as an ancestor by many of Rome's aristocratic families.

Romulus and Remus, Raised by Wolves

Despite the omens foretelling Aeneas as the founder of the Roman kingdom, it was his descendants, the twin brothers Romulus and Remus, that were credited with actually founding Rome. Romulus and Remus were born to Rhea Silvia, a descendant of Aeneas and princess of the city Aeneas's son Ascanio founded. Rhea Silvia was forced to become a vestal virgin when her uncle Amulius overthrew her father Numitor and took his throne. Amulius believed if Rhea were bound to chastity as a priestess of Vesta, she would never bear sons to threaten his rule.

In most versions of the story, Rhea did not willingly break her vestal vows but was raped, either by the god Mars or an unknown assailant. Rhea's claim that the father of her twins was Mars saved her life, as her uncle was afraid of bringing the wrath of the god, and therefore instead of being executed, Rhea was imprisoned. She gave birth to twins Romulus and Remus, who her uncle had ordered thrown into the river Tiber, but a servant took pity and placed them in a basket instead. The river god also took pity on them and sent the basket to the bottom of Palatine Hill, where it was discovered by a wolf who cared for them until human parents adopted them.

The symbolism in this story is strong. Rhea is often said to have been sleeping when Mars raped her, and in her sleep, she dreamed of two seeds that became trees that grew to envelop the whole world. Wolves were associated with Mars, so the wolf that saved the twins was seen as a sign that Mars protected his children. In some versions, another animal associated with Mars, the woodpecker, brings the children food.

Hercules, the Strongest Man in the World

Perhaps no other figure from Roman mythology has captured the modern imagination like Hercules, whose saga has inspired epic poems, long-running television shows, and even Disney movies. The same was true of his place in Roman culture, with some emperors even borrowing his traits (muscular, athletic body, armed with a club and wearing a lion pelt) when they had their own statues made. The Romans adapted Hercules from the Greek hero Heracles. It's possible that his cult was the first one to come into Rome from a foreign land. Though he was technically a demigod, he earned immortality upon his death, with one of Jupiter's lightning bolts striking his pyre and making him vanish. After this, he lived on Mt. Etna and worshipped as a god.

Hercules was born out of an affair between Jupiter and the mortal Alcmene, and his very existence was enraging to Jupiter's wife, Juno. Juno despised Hercules so much that she sent snakes to murder Hercules when he was just a baby, not knowing that he had god-like strength. Baby Hercules promptly strangled the snakes. In Juno's cruelest attack, she took advantage of his strength as well as his infamous temper, casting a spell that made Hercules go mad with rage. In this state, he murdered his wife Megara and their children. It was for this crime that he was given and willingly accepted the twelve heroic tasks that would test his strength and make him live forever, not only among the gods on Mt. Etna, but in history and popular imagination the world over.

Castor, Pollux, and Helen of Troy

While many people today might know of these three figures from Roman myth and history--Helen for her abduction by the prince of Troy and the war that resulted from that abduction, Castor and Pollux as the twin fighters represented in the constellation Gemini--it is less well-known that these three were siblings. In some renditions, all three are the children of Jupiter, who seduced their mother, Latona. The story of their conception is strange even by mythological standards, as Jupiter was a swan at the time, and Latona gave birth via eggs. More commonly, however, only Helen and Pollux were Jupiter's children, while Castor was conceived on the same night as Pollux but by their mother's mortal husband, Tyndareus, King of Sparta.

Helen was known for her beauty, which honestly brought her as much trouble as it did glory. While Helen was most famously stolen away by Paris (by some accounts willingly, by others not), this was not her first kidnapping. When she was younger, she was taken by the Athenian Theseus, who wanted her for his wife. Fortunately, Castor and Pollux came to Athens and rescued her. The brothers were renowned fighters and patrons of the Roman cavalry, with Castor, in particular, strongly associated with the equities (Rome's version of knights). Though their fighting skills helped save their sister, they eventually proved to be the twin's undoing, as a fight over either cattle or women (sources disagree) led to Castor's death. Protected by his divine paternity, Pollux was deeply grieved at the loss of Castor, so much so that he eventually convinced his father to allow him to share his immortality, each brother spending half their time in the living world and the other half in the underworld.

Brutus the Revolutionary and the Tragedy of Lucretia

In the sixth century B.C.E., Rome was still a kingdom. The Tarquins, the royal family at the time, were known to be corrupt, cruel, and generally terrible rulers, including Collantinus, whose wife, Lucretia, was known for her goodness and virtue. Sextus, one of the Tarquinian princes, was angry at the honor Lucretia brought to Collantinus, so he snuck into their home and raped Lucretia. Though a victim by today's standards, Roman law held women responsible for their assaults and branded them as adulterers. Rather than live with this, Lucretia killed herself, but not before extorting her husband and all the men present to redress her dishonor.

One of those men was Lucius Junius Brutus. Brutus is sometimes claimed as Lucretia's uncle, while other stories position him as her husband's friend. He was also said to be the king's nephew by marriage, but that did not stop him from swearing to bring retribution to the entire Tarquin family and then mercilessly following through. Lucretia's dead body was placed out for the public to see. Her choice of death over dishonor made her even more virtuous in the eyes of Rome's citizens and created a focal point for the population's dissatisfaction with the Tarquin's totalitarian rule. Capitalizing on the outrage over Lucretia's death, Brutus and Collantinus led the people of Rome in a revolt against the king and his family. After driving out the royal family, they declared Rome would never have a king again, and thus Rome became a republic.

Cloelia and Her Daring Escape

Cloelia was a contemporary of Brutus, and her story occurs not long after the suicide of Lucretia and the exile of the Tarquins. It begins when an Etruscan king named Lars Porsenna decides to lay siege to Rome. Unable to defeat Porsenna, Rome sued for peace, offering him a group of hostages as part of an attempt at a treaty. Cloelia was one of those hostages, and apparently an unwilling one, as she not only broke out of Porsenna's camp but took the other female hostages with her. The only route to Rome from camp was the River Tiber, and so the hostages swam across it. It was a courageous act that was futile in the end, as Rome promptly gave the hostages back to Porsenna. Porsenna was impressed with Cloelia's boldness and courage though, so he freed her and allowed her to choose other hostages to release as well. The more sentimental versions of the story have Cloelia freeing young children to keep them from harm, while the perhaps more characteristically Roman versions have her choosing the best fighters so that Rome could continue to withstand Porsenna's siege.

Many of Rome's historians cite Cloelia's bravery as having influenced Porsenna to withdraw his attack. Historically speaking, there is some doubt about this. Rather than ceding his advantage because the courage of Rome moved him, it is very possible Porsenna did conquer Rome but chose not to rule it as king. In doing so, he would have been another figure that was instrumental in establishing Rome's republic. But that version of events lacks the victorious and heroic qualities that Romans preferred to find in their history. And so, Cloelia's story remains a testament to a Roman ideal that was very dearly held even if not historically accurate.

Marcus Curtius, Rome's Precious Possession

In addition to illustrating Roman valor, some heroic tales also sought to explain natural disasters or illuminate the history behind archaic sites. The story of Marcus Curtius does all three, as it involves a fearless young soldier, the remnants of a pond in the middle of Rome, and an ancient earthquake. The pond, now filled and covered with stone, is called the Lacus Curtius, Latin for "Lake of Curtius." The legend goes that a great rift opened up on this spot in the fourth century B.C.E., threatening to swallow the whole city. As with any situation, Romans consulted the gods to determine what they might do to regain divine favor and save their city. According to the Roman historian Titus Livius, the oracle responded that the only way to save Rome was to throw into the abyss the thing that the city held most dear, *"quo plurimum populus Romanus posset."*

Upon hearing this, most of the population despaired--who could say what Rome held most dear, let alone part with it? But Marcus Curtius, a proud Roman soldier, believed that Rome's treasure was her military might and that he was its perfect embodiment. He, therefore, put on his armor, got on his horse, and leaped into the fissure. The rift closed, and Rome survived. The Lacus Curtius is supposedly named after this sacrificial act and can still be visited in Rome today. Marcus Curtius himself became a popular subject for artists, who usually depict him mid-leap in all his martial, self-sacrificing glory.

Spartacus, the Slave Who Led a Rebellion

Fighting was a way of life in the Roman Empire, and in that sense, there is no more Roman a hero than Spartacus. Had his life gone a different way, he might have found glory as a famous Roman soldier, as most historians suspect that he served in the Roman army at some point early in his career. Instead of rising through the ranks, however, Spartacus was sold into slavery. It's unknown why or how this happened, though a failed attempt to flee from or rebel against military service is one possible reason. His new master was a teacher at an institution that trained gladiators and, perhaps unwisely, chose to train Spartacus there. This backfired almost immediately, as within the year, Spartacus formed a trio with two fellow gladiators, and together they led a breakout. Unluckily for the Romans they encountered, they were successful in escaping and managed to steal weapons as they went.

This group of former gladiators camped out near Mt. Vesuvius, and when other slaves heard about them, they started joining Spartacus and his group of rebels. These former slaves fought off the Roman army for almost a year while their numbers continued to swell, possibly growing as large as 100,000 men. After gaining strength, the slave army began marching north, out of Italy, and into modern-day Europe. Initially, dealing with this rebellion was considered a local problem. But it gradually became apparent to Roman leaders that Spartacus and those with him had enough training and skills to pose a real threat. By this point, Spartacus and his army had begun moving back south, perhaps toward Sicily, intending to sail away from Italy or perhaps, more ambitiously, to attack Rome itself. Wherever they were going, they never made it and were finally overpowered near Naples, with Spartacus rumored to have been killed in battle along with many of his followers. Though technically Spartacus stood against Rome, his story became legendary in Roman history and later throughout the world.

Julius Caesar, the Engineer of the Empire

Rome remained a republic from the time of Brutus and Lucretia until Julius Caesar--perhaps the most famous Roman of all time--began to gain power. Caesar had both military prowess and political acumen. He lost no time climbing toward the top of Roman society, becoming a general and winning posts in Rome's territories before returning to Rome and becoming consul (the highest public official). Caesar is firmly established in our collective consciousness as a military hero ("I came, I saw, I conquered") and a victim of assassination and betrayal ("*Et tu, Brute?*"). He had a number of other accomplishments beyond these events, including creating a calendar system that Rome (and much of the places it occupied) would use for 1,500 years. His *Acta Diurna*, an announcement posted at the Roman forum detailing the government's actions, is considered a prototype for newspapers. He was even kidnapped by pirates once (he manipulated them and eventually orchestrated their demise at the hands of the Roman navy).

However, it is impossible to separate Julius Caesar from his most significant impact: the changing of Rome from a republic to an empire. While he was alive, his policies and military battles, including a civil war that he instigated and won, did much to alter the shape of Rome. But it was proclaiming himself dictator of Rome, an event that led to his death, that changed Roman history. Though Julius Caesar did not live to be Rome's first emperor, his chosen successor Octavian did, becoming Caesar Augustus and ushering in the era of the Roman Empire. He also became a symbol to the Roman populace and was eventually deified.

Ovid, the Collector of Stories

Ovid is something of an outlier in this chapter. He was not the child of a god, and he earned no military glory. In fact, he spent a good portion of his life exiled from Rome, having gotten on the wrong side of the emperor Augustus. Though Ovid's father hoped his sons would become prominent public officials, Ovid was not a statesman. Instead, he was a poet. He was not just any poet, though. He was incredibly popular among the patrician class in Rome, who loved his refined style and amorous subject matter. In his later life, he also wrote the epic poem *The Metamorphoses*, which attempted to tell the entire story of civilization. It included tales of gods and men, kingdoms and gallant deeds, and Ovid's most famous poem. In fact, the book was so influential among medieval writers that a period in the twelfth century was named "the Ovidian age" due to the number of poets who were copying Ovid's hexametrical style.

Ovid is also known to have influenced other famous poets, including Chaucer and Shakespeare (who wrote his own stories about Rome with his plays *Julius Caesar* and *Antony & Cleopatra*). You could say Ovid's greatest contribution to Rome's legacy was his artistry, or perhaps the way he wove mythology and history together in *The Metamorphoses*. Or you could point out that Ovid's poetry often took as its subject small, human things, like his poems about love or his piece "Fasti" on festival days. In these poems, Ovid preserved slices of everyday life in the Roman Empire. So even though he did not win battles or ascend to the mountain of the gods, in his way, Ovid was even more responsible than those heroes for the Roman Empire's renown, not just while it thrived but for centuries to come.

Chapter Four: Hair Made of Snakes
Mystical and Magical Beings in Roman Myths

Gods and heroes are always impressive, but if you've been waiting for something even more fantastic--or just for things to get weird--this chapter is for you. Again, borrowing extensively from Greek mythology before it, Roman mythology had a whole host of otherworldly creatures. Some could pass for human at a casual glance, while others were literal embodiments of elemental forces. They were frequently strange, occasionally grotesque, and always fascinating.

Stories about these creatures were good for more than just dinner party anecdotes, however. They often strove to make sense of nature and its phenomenon and help explain away aberrations and interruptions to the neat and orderly way that Romans preferred to structure their world. Try as they might, Romans could not always control everything that happened. Giving names and backstories to these things helped Romans find a sense of control, as well as comfort themselves with the idea that their heroes had also faced the monstrosities lurking in the wild and dangerous world.

Titans, the First Gods

The Titans were the children of Uranus and Gaea and were essentially the gods that came before the Roman gods that most people know. The previous chapters introduced one titan: Saturn, who overthrew his father Uranus and then ruled until his son Jupiter overthrew him. There were twelve titans originally, often associated with natural objects like the sun, the ocean, or abstract ideas like time and memory. Except for Jupiter and other gods who became part of the established pantheon, the children of the titans were also called titans.

Among these second-generation titans were recognizable figures such as Atlas and Prometheus.

There were two major stories involving the original titans. The first is their rebellion against their father, Uranus, who forced their mother Gaea to keep them locked in a dark pit called Tartarus (not only a place but also a being) until they liberated themselves. The second was their battle against Jupiter and the gods of his generation, which supposedly raged for a decade before the titans were finally defeated and banished back to Tartarus. The triumph of Jupiter and the other gods over the titans was seen as a victory for order over chaos. Fittingly, stories like that of second-generation titan Prometheus gifting fire to humankind against Jupiter's wishes can be read as both the titans and the natural elements they represented continuing their defiance against the imposed decorum of the gods.

Typhon, Father of Monsters

Another of Gaea's children, Typhon was not fathered by Uranus but by Tartarus (yes, *that Tartarus*, the dark pit in the center of the underworld). Some accounts have Jupiter defeating Typhon and throwing him back to Tartarus, while others claim that Jupiter lit him on fire and, when that didn't kill him, buried him alive in the earth under Mt. Etna. This imprisonment was sometimes said to be the cause of Mt. Etna's eruptions.

Typhon had a truly terrible appearance, described as having 100 heads, all of which not only resembled snakes and breathed fire, but made a cacophony of sounds as if every known animal was making noise at once. Some portrayals also give him wings. He was the mate of the half-serpent half-woman Echidna. Their children include some of the most fearsome monsters in mythology, including Pluto's multi-headed guard dog Cerberus and two of the monsters defeated by Hercules, the Hydra and the Ladon. Their infamous offspring earned

Typhon and Echidna the titles "father and mother of monsters." Typhon is immortalized in our modern language in the word "typhoon."

Gorgons, Who Froze You in Fear

The most famous of the gorgons is Medusa, who was slain and beheaded by the hero Perseus, but she was not the only gorgon in Roman mythology. There were three gorgons: Medusa and her sisters, Stheno and Euryale. Physical descriptions of the gorgons vary by source, but all of them agree on two points: they had hair of live snakes, and they were in some way grotesque. This grotesquery was usually due to a slew of inhuman body parts, including wings, fangs, claws, scales, tusks, and sometimes compounded by the ugliness of their faces. Another characteristic universally known was their ability to turn people to stone with the power of their stare.

Medusa was set apart from her sisters with claims that she was the only mortal gorgon, sometimes believed to retain a beautiful human face, and of course, because she was the one famously killed. Even in death, a gorgon could bring about extraordinary things. Depending on which side you drew from, it was believed that their blood was either deadly poison or a potion for resurrection. And when Medusa's head was cut off, a winged horse (the famed Pegasus) flew out of it. In fact, Perseus took Medusa's head and set it on her shield so that its glare, still potent even when lifeless, could ward off enemies. Depictions of gorgons were placed on houses for this exact reason.

Nymphs, Your Friendly Neighborhood Nature Spirit

Nymphs are ubiquitous throughout Greek and Roman mythology, evidenced by how they have already appeared several times in this book. Remember that Syrinx, who was pursued by Faunus and turned into pan pipes, was a nymph. Also, unnamed nymphs were the caretakers of young Aeneas in the hills of Mt. Ida and among the followers of Bacchus. Diana, another nature goddess, was also known to keep company with nymphs. Nymphs were not immortal like the gods, but they did live for a very long time. They were known for two things: their distracting beauty and their connection to the natural world. Nymphs were exclusively female and eternally young, meant to represent the female connection with life and procreation. Though generally benevolent, they were often accused of seducing men or driving them mad with longing. On the other hand, if a nymph became enamored with a mortal, they were rumored to become aggressive if their affections were rejected and sometimes would abduct young men who had taken their fancy.

Nymphs were often depicted as having adolescent personalities, equally passionate in their joys and indulgences as they were in their anger and heartbreak. The earliest nymphs were probably local deities attached to bodies of water, which rural communities built shrines to and would leave offerings for (usually some type of animal sacrifice). This practice of placing an offering at a water shrine evolved over the centuries but never completely disappeared. Its modern-day echo can be seen in the ritual of tossing coins into a fountain.

Satyrs, Rough and Rowdy Troublemakers

Satyrs were the male counterparts to nymphs and had many associations with the natural world and nature gods like Bacchus. They also bore a resemblance to Faunus, having a half-human, half-animal appearance like him. Satyrs were common in both Greek and Roman mythology. While Greek tradition usually depicted them as men with the ears and the tail of a horse, in Roman myth they had the bottom half of a goat and horns on their (otherwise human) heads. Satyrs were rural gods known to live in forests and mountains. Their wild nature reflected this, as they were known to misbehave in playful and malicious ways, sometimes pursuing and harassing nymphs or getting drunk and causing trouble.

Their reputation wasn't all bad, however. They could be quite hard-working if they wanted--a trait Bacchus put to good use when he engaged them to make wine--and they were often musically inclined. They were also believed to be intelligent and could be keepers of essential knowledge. One of the most well-known satyrs, Silenus, was a teacher, with Bacchus being his most famous pupil. So, while the modern legacy of satyrs seems to be their lusty nature (the Oxford dictionary's secondary definition for satyr reads "a man who has strong sexual desires," their original natures were more complex. These paradoxical character traits, to be primitive and live with abandon while also capable of being wise and productive, perhaps reflected the kind of nuance and diversity found in the natural world they represented.

Scylla, Devouring Sailors with Her Six Dog Heads

Scylla and her neighbor Charybdis (more on her in the next entry) are mythological creatures who lived in a real place, the Straits of Messina, a precarious watery passage between the tip of Italy and the island of Sicily. Scylla lived in the cliffs around the straits, and she was a woman, sort of--she also possessed six extra heads, each a fearsome dog with rows of sharp teeth in its mouth. She used these heads to reach out from her lair and snatch men from ships as they sailed by.

Scylla's origin story is murky. In some versions, she is the daughter of spirits, gods, or titans (like Typhon). In contrast, in later versions, she is a mortal woman or a sea nymph whose romantic relationship with Neptune provoked the jealousy of one of Neptune's other lovers (usually the sorceress Circe or the sea goddess Amphitrite), causing them to curse her with a new, monstrous form. Her name, appropriately, might come from the word *skyllein*, which means "to tear." In some accounts, she cannot speak, but only bark or whine like a dog. Even after sailors stopped believing in the story of Scylla, the fierce dog-headed monster, they still spoke in fear of a rock in the Straits of Messina that was known to sink ships, also called Scylla.

Charybdis, the Whirlpool Who Left No Survivors

Across the Straits of Messina from Scylla's cliffside cave lay Charybdis, less a creature than an elemental force of nature. By most accounts, the child of Neptune and Gaea, Charybdis was initially a nymph before she was turned into a whirlpool by Jupiter. In some versions of her story, Jupiter was displeased with her lascivious nature and struck her with one of his lightning bolts, banishing her to the depths of the sea. In other versions, Jupiter sent her into the sea after she was caught trying to steal cows from Hercules. Regardless of the reason, the result was that she became part of the straits itself, a whirling vortex even more dangerous to passing ships than Scylla.

With Charybdis on one side of the straits and Scylla on the other, the passage was perhaps one of Roman mythology's most dangerous heroic trials. However, the difference in power was clear--Scylla would take six of your men with her six heads, while Charybdis would take your whole ship. And once you were caught in Charybdis' grasp, there was no chance of escape. Odysseus was famously advised to avoid Charybdis at all costs, even if that meant some of his sailors were eaten by Scylla. (He ended up encountering both and only surviving through divine intervention.) This hero's dilemma, to navigate between two terrifying forces that could only be endured and escaped but never conquered, created the phrase *"between Scylla and Charybdis,"* the Roman mythological equivalent of *"between a rock and a hard place."*

The Fates, Weavers of Destiny

The fates were, rather obviously, beings that controlled the fate of everyone and everything. They are usually depicted as a group of three women, often older, engaged in spinning thread. Each thread represented an individual lifeline, and each of the three had their part to play in the spinning--usually, one to hold the unspun thread, one to weave, and one to cut the thread when a life was meant to end. They went by other names as well, including the Moirai ("those who allot") and the Keres ("those who cut off"). Because they were believed to set the course of someone's entire life, they were thought to be present at every birth and, therefore, sometimes linked to the act of birth itself.

Specifically in Roman culture, they were known as the Fates Parcae, which means "those who bring forth the child." Two of the Fates Parcae (Nona and Decuma) started as Roman goddesses of childbearing; to these two, a third goddess, Morta, was added when the Romans assimilated the Greek idea of the Fates as a trio of goddesses. The names of Nona and Decima reflect their origins, referring to birth at nine months and ten months, respectively. Morta was taken to mean death resulting in a still-born child. Among all the beings in this book, the fates alone could claim they were more powerful even than the gods themselves, as they were the ones who doled out powers and had the final say in any being's destiny.

The Furies, Avenging Demons

The furies were created from the blood of Uranus when he was overthrown by the titans, in the same way as Venus. However, while Venus was born when his blood fell in the ocean, the furies were born when his blood fell onto the earth. (An alternate beginning suggests they were the daughters of the night goddess Nox.) It was the furies' job to bring a reckoning to wrongdoers, particularly if they had broken promises or hurt someone's family. They were known as defenders of older family or community members and for those shunned by society. The furies were popular in the epic poems of ancient Rome, including *The Metamorphoses* and *The Aeneid*.

Like the fates, the furies had other names, the Semnai ("the majestic ones," referencing their extraordinary powers) and the Eumenides ("the kindly ones," hinting at the gratitude of those whom they avenged). They could be called upon using curses, and their wrath took many forms, including striking their targets with sickness or insanity. When they caught a culprit, they often hauled them to the underworld. Their physical presence was nearly as alarming as their powers. They had black skin and bat-like wings, with snakes in their hair and whips or cups of poison in their hands. Their arrival was marked by storms, bugs, and a terrible smell. The Romans, however, with their sense of order, did not consider the furies villains, but rather as a necessary part of a just civilization, who need not be feared by those who behaved as they should.

The Graces, Bearers of Beauty and Charm

Like so many others, the graces were children of Jupiter, usually with the ocean nymph Eurynome, but occasionally with Juno. Initially known only as a group, in later stories, they were sometimes given individual names, and at times they were represented as a group of three, just as with the fates and the furies. The graces were depicted as young women, often partially or entirely naked, holding hands and sometimes dancing (as they were known to dance for the amusement of the gods).

They were meant to embody grace and charm and were tasked with spreading happiness, giving blessings, and encouraging festivity. They were also said to bring beauty to the world and were linked with the blooming of flowers in springtime. With these characteristics, it only makes sense that they were also associated with Venus and Cupid. In some traditions, Vulcan's wife is not Venus, but the youngest of the graces, Aglaea. They are also sometimes connected or even conflated with the muses, who were responsible for artistic inspiration. While they were not often major characters or protagonists in Roman mythology, they were frequently big players in the stories of more prominent heroes or deities.

Chapter Five: Impossible Tasks and Magnificent Champions
Famous Stories from Roman Mythology

So far, this book has mainly concerned itself with the who's who of ancient Rome, the bold and extraordinary personalities that populated Roman mythology, be they divine, human, or somewhere in between. But these entries often condensed the exploits of their subjects into a sentence or two, and there are some stories from Roman mythology that are worth a more detailed telling. In these stories, you'll find many familiar faces, but some new names as well. All of them, whether strange, harrowing, mystical, or heroic, had some brush with fate that made their tales stick in the imaginations of the Roman people and often in our modern imaginations as well.

The Many Voyages of Aeneas

As already established, we know the story of Aeneas very well because Virgil made him the subject of his famous poem, *The Aeneid*. With *The Aeneid*, Virgil wanted to create the sort of epic story that Greek heroes were known for, and so he shaped Aeneas's tale to mirror that of Odysseus in Homer's *The Iliad* and *The Odyssey*. When Aeneas and his men fled Troy, they initially went to Mt. Ida, where Aeneas had been born and where he lived as a child under the care of the mountain nymphs that dwelled there. Here the Trojans rested and built ships so they could continue their journey. This is where *The Aeneid* starts, the first half of the poem being about Aeneas and the other surviving Trojans wandering around the Mediterranean, while the second half is about the war that they engaged in once they finally made it to Italy.

Once Aeneas and his men begin their voyage to Italy, they lose their way in a storm and land on the shores of Carthage. There, at the court of Queen Dido, Aeneas recounts how he and his men came to land in Africa after they escaped from Troy. Dido had her own odyssey, originally a queen of the Phoenician city of Tyre, before she and her subjects were forced to flee after the murder of her husband. (It is worth noting that this meeting between Aeneas and Dido is a factual impossibility, as Carthage was founded centuries after the fall of Troy, so even if Aeneas and Dido were both actual people, they would not have been alive at the same time.) According to *The Aeneid*, no suitor could tempt the widowed Dido until Aeneas showed up, at which point Cupid, at the behest of Venus, struck Dido with an arrow that made her love Aeneas. (Alternatively, Cupid was sent by Juno, who was nursing several grudges against the Trojans and was furious that Aeneas and his followers survived.)

Jupiter, intervening, presumably because the existence of Rome itself hung in the balance, then sent Mercury to admonish Aeneas for falling in love and forgetting that destiny waited for him in Italy. Aeneas gathered his men and left, breaking Dido's heart and leading her to curse them and commit suicide by hurling herself onto a burning pyre. Finally making it to Italy, Aeneas was taken on his most fantastical journey yet, as the Apollonian priestess Sibyl escorted him to the underworld. Awkwardly, many of the men Aeneas has killed are there, as is Dido. Most crucially for our story, however, Aeneas meets his father Anchises, who paints a vivid picture of the legendary place that their family will found.

Newly focused after his trip through the underworld and his chat with his dead father, Aeneas found aid in the Italian kingdom of Latium, where King Latinus not only gave land to the Trojans but his blessing for Aeneas to marry his daughter Lavinia. Lavinia's mother preferred a different suitor, however, being King Turnus of the Rutuli. The conflict between the two admirers eventually escalated into a full-fledged war. This war continued until Venus convinced her husband Vulcan to give Aeneas specially made armor (no mean feat, considering that Aeneas was her child by another man). Thus armed, Aeneas was able to defeat Turnus, marry Lavinia, and finally establish a stable, peaceful kingdom for the Trojans. Later, Aeneas's descendent, Ascanius, would leave this kingdom to establish Alba Longa, where Romulus and Remus would be born.

The Founding of Rome

Had the story of Romulus and Remus ended when they were rescued and adopted by a shepherd on Palatine Hill, it would have still been extraordinary. They were already children of a god, born to an imprisoned princess, saved from a watery death by a servant never named, and nursed through infancy by a particularly maternal wolf. But it turns out that all that was just a prologue. Because a shepherd adopted them, Romulus and Remus also grew up to be shepherds. While tending their flock, they encountered shepherds for their mother's uncle, King Amulius (who, you may remember, ordered their execution and thought they were dead). These shepherds started a fight, and in the end, Remus was captured and taken back to their birthplace of Alba Longa. Romulus followed to free his brother, at which point they decided it was time for the king's reign to end. Together they killed him and put their grandfather, King Numitor, back on the throne. In some stories, Numitor is instrumental in overthrowing his brother and taking back his crown. In others, Remus and Romulus are asked to be kings by the people of Alba Longa, but they refuse and reinstate their grandfather instead.

Having set things right in their birthplace, Romulus and Remus returned to where they grew up, now wishing to start their own kingdom. The two brothers traveled through what was known as the seven hills, but unfortunately, they disagreed on where it was best to build their city. Romulus argued for Palatine Hill, while Remus argued for Aventine Hill. Or, in some versions, the disagreement is over the name of the city. They decide to leave the decision up to the gods by looking for omens in the birds flying overhead but can't agree on the meanings of the omens either. Remus sees six birds first, while Romulus sees twelve birds total, the former arguing it was he who saw the birds first that won, and the latter arguing it was the highest number of birds.

Irritated with their disagreement, Romulus decided he would not wait for Remus to change his mind and began to build on his chosen hill. He started with a wall, which Remus, in true brotherly fashion, decided to mock by jumping over it. What happened next is disputed: some stories say Romulus was so angry with Remus that he killed him, while others (including St. Jerome) say it was not Romulus but one of his followers that killed Remus. The Roman historian Titus Livius proposes that the jump itself killed Remus, a sign that he had fallen out of favor with the gods. Whatever the exact cause, all agree that the clash ended with Remus dead and Romulus left to found the city of Rome where and how he pleased, naming it after himself.

After founding the city, Romulus became its first king and ruled over it for 40 years. When his grandfather Numitor died, Romulus inherited that throne and added Alba Longa to his kingdom, the first acquisition of the Roman Empire. Just as with Remus, there are competing versions of Romulus's death, ranging from the very mundane suggestion that the senate he established eventually wished him out of the way and orchestrated his murder to the fantastical tale that a whirlwind took him up directly into heaven. Whether Romulus met the very human fate of being stabbed in the back or the divine one of becoming a god (and whether Romulus existed in history as Rome's actual first leader, or just in myth as its demigod architect), his name and his story, along with his brother, are still remembered today.

The Twelve Tasks of Hercules

After Hercules tragically killed his family under the influence of Juno's spell, he begged the god Apollo to give him a way to atone for his actions. Apollo charged him to complete twelve tasks assigned to him by a king named Eurystheus. Many of these undertakings were thought to be impossible, but Hercules accomplished them all, earning not only his contrition but a place among the gods on Mt. Etna.

The First Task: The Nemean Lion

The people of Nemea were being stalked and killed by a ferocious lion, so Eurystheus asked Hercules to find it and get rid of it. Hercules tracked the lion to its cave, where he reportedly choked the life out of it with his bare hands. Depictions of Hercules frequently showed him wearing a cape made from the Nemean lion's hide.

The Second Task: The Hydra

The hydra was a poisonous creature with many heads (usually nine) that lived in Lake Lerna, one of the entrances to the underworld. It was difficult to kill because for every head cut off, two more grew. Hercules solved this by bringing his nephew, who cauterized each neck as soon as Hercules removed its head.

The Third Task: Diana's Golden Deer

King Eurystheus, obviously not invested in Hercules's success, next sent him after the beloved sacred deer of the goddess Diana, known for its golden antlers. Catching the deer was the easy part. However, it was thought anyone hunting it would incur Diana's wrath.

But when Hercules told Diana his tragic backstory, she was moved to leniency and allowed him to live.

The Fourth Task: The Man-Eating Boar

Unfortunately, a boar living on Mt. Erymanthus had developed a taste for human flesh, and Hercules was sent to capture it. Perhaps by this point, Hercules was very practiced at subduing horrific beasts, as this task didn't seem to have him breaking a sweat. He used a large net to capture the boar.

The Fifth Task: The Stables of King Augeas

Next, Hercules was asked to clean out the stables of a king called Augeas. This might seem small compared to his first four tasks, but it was actually particularly tricky. The stables were huge, and Hercules would only succeed if he could clean them in one day. Fortunately, Hercules worked smart and not hard, redirecting a couple of rivers to wash through the stables.

The Sixth Task: Birds Worthy of Hitchcock

A town called Stymphalos had developed something of an infestation--it was plagued by many, many birds (by some accounts, carnivorous ones). For his sixth task, Hercules was sent to get rid of them. Luckily for Hercules, Minerva decided to help him out, gifting him with a pair of noisy clappers made by Vulcan that he was able to use to scare the birds away.

The Seventh Task: A Bull Gone Wild

Halfway through his tasks, Hercules next went to Crete to apprehend a bull that was causing quite a bit of chaos. Among other things, it had gotten into a romantic relationship with the king's wife and gotten her pregnant. This bull was said to be exceptionally magnificent, which is perhaps why instead of killing it, Hercules herded it into King Eurystheus's possession.

The Eighth Task: The Four Horses of Diomedes

Next, journeying to Thrace, Hercules confronted a quartet of horses that belonged to the king, Diomedes. Although these horses had started eating people, Hercules again spared them and brought them to King Eurystheus. However, Diomedes was not so lucky and was killed in combat by Hercules.

The Ninth Task: The Amazonian Belt

For his ninth task, Hercules was again sent to steal something from a woman, this time a belt from Hippolyte, the queen of the Amazons. Hercules initially charmed Hippolyte as he had Diana, but Juno, who felt he'd been having too easy of a time thus far, started a rumor among the Amazons that Hercules meant the queen harm. When the Amazons attacked him, Hercules took drastic measures, murdering Hippolyte and escaping with her belt.

The Tenth Task: A Troublesome Herd of Cattle

There were many disturbing things about the cows Hercules had to steal for his tenth task, starting with how they were owned by a monster with three heads, Geryon, who lived on a faraway island. After reaching the island and killing Geryon, Hercules had to bring all the cows back. Ultimately, he was successful, but he was plagued by missing cows, thieves, and more meddlesome interference from Juno.

The Eleventh Task: Juno's Golden Apples

As if Juno didn't hate him enough already, Hercules next had to rob Jupiter of the golden apples that Juno had given him when they married. Once again, friends in high places came through, as Hercules got titans Prometheus and Atlas to help him. Perhaps aware that he was tempting fate, once Hercules proved that he had stolen the apples, he quickly returned them.

The Twelfth Task: Dognapping Cerberus

For his final task, Hercules had to steal another prized possession from another god, this time being Pluto's three-headed hound, Cerberus. Hercules was able to drag Cerberus from the underworld because of his immense strength and, once again, wisely returned what he had stolen once the task was accomplished.

The Minotaur's Labyrinth

While the story of the minotaur originated in Greece, it was the Romans who recorded the most detailed narratives about him, including Ovid's *Metamorphoses*. The minotaur was the child that the Cretan bull (yes, the one Hercules captured) had with the Queen of Crete, Pasiphae. While its name was Asterion, it became known by its association with its adopted father, King Minos--minotaur means "Minos's bull." The minotaur's father came to Crete from the ocean when King Minos asked Pluto to provide a sign that the gods favored his ascension to the throne, and Pluto sent a beautiful bull from the sea as proof. In some versions, the queen's desire for the bull is a punishment from Pluto, as Minos promised he would sacrifice the bull to Pluto and then reneged, letting the bull live. In others, the punishment comes from Venus, who felt Pasiphae had slacked in her adoration.

Born of a woman and a bull, the minotaur had the head and tail of a bull and the body of a man (a reversal from the more common mythological hybrid of a human head on an animal body). Unfortunately, as the minotaur grew, it no longer could eat regular food and instead began eating people, causing Minos to ask his craftsman Daedalus to build a labyrinth in which the minotaur would be lost forever. Unwilling to feed his own people to the minotaur, Minos looked to the Athenians, who he held responsible for the death of his son. King Minos cursed Athens, lifting the curse only when the city agreed to a regular tribute of young people to be fed to the minotaur.

While this worked for a while, eventually, an Athenian named Theseus decided he would end this slaughter of Athens' youth by killing the minotaur. You may remember Theseus from trying to kidnap Helen, a slightly less heroic act. Once in Crete, Theseus made an ally of the king's daughter Ariadne, using her obvious affection for him to get her help in navigating the labyrinth. Ariadne, sometimes aided by Daedalus, realized that Theseus could find his way out of the labyrinth if he carried one end of a string and she held onto the other end at the labyrinth's entrance. And so Theseus found and killed the minotaur and then fled Crete, taking Ariadne with him.

While the story of the minotaur is obviously mythical, there is some suggestion that Crete did have a Minos--or several--as the word minos is believed to be a title used for Crete's ruler. And while there is no archaeological evidence for a labyrinth in Crete, some historians have proposed that the term might have initially referred to the Cretan palace and that the stories of a bull that ate people came from ritual sacrifices made by a priest dressed as a bull.

Arachne, Minerva, and the Weaving Contest

It may seem anticlimactic to end with a story about weaving, but Arachne did something as bold as any of the warriors or demigods found in this book--she challenged a god. Specifically, she got so good at weaving that she claimed she was a better weaver than Minerva, the goddess of craftsmen. Minerva, of course, could not let this stand, and the two engaged in a weaving contest. According to Ovid, who wrote about the contest in *Metamorphoses*, Minerva's tapestry had two themes: the powers of the gods and the terrible fates that befell mortals who dared to confront them. Arachne, apparently unintimidated, chose an opposing theme: stories in which gods had abused their powers to deceive and harm mortals.

By all accounts, Arachne's weaving was superior to Minerva's. Some versions of the story say that Minerva ignored this fact and proclaimed herself the victor anyway, before turning Arachne into a spider. Other versions, including Ovid's, paint Minerva as a very sore loser who rips up the cloth Arachne has woven and then starts beating her with a weaving shuttle, causing Arachne to hang herself in the weaving threads. Minerva then regrets her anger and saves Arachne from dying by turning her into a spider.

A simple reading of this story might suggest the moral is that you should never challenge a god, as even garnering their compassion can leave you stuck as a bug for the rest of your life. However, you could also make a more nuanced assessment of the story. In one particularly compelling argument, the Colby College Center for the Arts and Humanities offers a direct comparison between the story of Arachne and its most famous teller, Ovid. Like Arachne, Ovid was known to have challenged a powerful figure (the Roman emperor Augustus), and like Arachne, Ovid lost the challenge and, to some extent, his life (as he was kicked out of Rome). However, just as Arachne kept spinning even as a spider, Ovid wrote, even in exile.

This interpretation hints at the complexity found in Roman mythology and any mythology or set of tales. Sometimes, perhaps always, the person telling the story is just as much a part of the narrative as the story itself.

Final Words

Though this book has covered much of Roman mythology--from the heights of Mt. Etna to the depths of the underworld; to the founding of Rome to the poets who preserved its legacy--there is still much more to explore. Hopefully, reading about these gods, goddesses, heroes, monsters, and daring tales has inspired you to learn more and to dive deeper into the depths of this rich cultural pool. Just be careful not to get too close to Charybdis!

Or perhaps, having sampled Roman mythology, now you're wondering about the myths and history of other ancient civilizations. Maybe you're motivated to look into Greek myths, to compare them to their Roman counterparts, or gain a different perspective on ancient Mediterranean civilizations. Or you might like to follow the caesars and gods that journeyed into Africa, where you could dip your toe into Egyptian mythology. Or you could journey farther still, to other parts of the world, discovering Norse mythology and Scandinavia or Celtic mythology from the British Isles. If you are interested in any of these mythologies, I have multiple books available covering these topics that can be found on Amazon and through a variety of book retailers.

Then again, you might step away from considering the past to think about how these stories still resonate in the present. After all, themes of power and desire, conflict and creation, are just as relevant in today's world as they were two millennia ago.

Whether you see these stories as history, allegory, entertainment, or some mix of the three, hopefully, this book has given you a glimpse of what it meant to be a part of Ovid's everyday present, which is now our long-ago past. And hopefully, you can take a little of that past with you into your everyday life, even if it's just to throw a coin into a fountain every once in a while.

www.ingramcontent.com/pod-product-compliance
Lightning Source LLC
LaVergne TN
LVHW021739060526
838200LV00052B/3374